T0171602

Broken Vessels Can Be Mended

By
Aurie

authorHOUSE®

AuthorHouse™
1663 Liberty Drive
Bloomington, IN 47403
www.authorhouse.com
Phone: 1-800-839-8640

First published by AuthorHouse 04/01/2011

ISBN: 978-1-4520-4457-6 (sc)
ISBN: 978-1-4520-4458-3 (e)

Library of Congress Control Number 2010917934

Printed in the United States of America

Acknowledgements

This book would not have been possible had there not been a God who loves and cares for his own.

And it is His greatest pleasure to help His creation when they have no where else to turn, but many times He uses frail creatures to carry out His work.

He put us on this earth together for that reason, so we can help each other, and by doing so, glorify the Creator.

And only when we live like Him, can we love those around us and "lift up the hands that hang down."

With that said, I would like to say a heart felt thank you to the "specials" in my life that taught me to fly, when I didn't think I even had wings.

First of all to Chet and Carol, you were the ones who got me through some of the toughest years of my life. You put up with me and cared when I was the most obnoxious. I'll be forever grateful for the many hours you spent sitting and listening to me, when I know you had much better things to do. The many times you included me in your family are special memories I'll always cherish.

Uncle Paul and Aunt Rose, the eight months I spent with you will always be among the best of my life. You shared your home and your life unselfishly, and opened my eyes to a way of life I had not experienced before. Thank you from the bottom of my heart!

To Uriah and Karen for all the many hours on the phone helping me work through the memories that threatened to overwhelm me. Thank you!

To my big sister, I could never have made it without you. Sometimes only family understands the implications of memories of events and places. You always were there and cared. Even though you were nine years older than me you've been the perfect big sis. Thank you a thousand times!

And to my children, — what would I ever have done without you! You were my reason to go on when I had no other reason left.

To my oldest daughter, you have been my strength. So many times I didn't have the energy left to care for your brother and sister, or to be the mediator in their squabbles and you jumped in and filled the place I should have been filling. Please accept my sincerest apologies for the fact you had to shoulder responsibilities that should have been mine. And through it all you have grown to be a beautiful person, I love with all my heart and I hope that God rewards you especially for the part you've played in my healing!

To my only son, the one who always knew when I was hurting and to the best of your ability, you tried to lift the load. Your sensitivity and caring smoothed the rough times and were an anchor when I wanted to fly away from it all. God made you a caretaker and a leader, and someday some lucky young lady will be thrilled to make a home for you! May you be worthy of each other!

To my youngest, my angel the one who is always there when I need a hug! You are a very special girl; your ability to just sit quietly and read or sometimes talk, have been a balm when things were particularly hard. Your Imagination lightens the load when you can see the humor in situations! Thank you for being you, and not being too big to sit on my lap and give me a hug, I love you, girl!

And to my Husband, the one God gave me. He knew just what I needed in a mate. Some one resilient enough to hold up under the stress of a life with a ruined, broken, vessel. And strong enough to stand by while that same vessel was put back on the potter's wheel and mended. I'm so sorry for all the pain I've caused you, the years of misunderstandings.

All the sleepless nights and the messy house when I couldn't function. Your sense of humor has been our salvation so many times, when things looked too hopeless, you always managed to see the funny side. Thank you! And if God grants us years together yet, I hope I can make up to you a little of the pain I've put you through. I love you with all my heart and I'd like the chance to prove it!

And to all the other friends who've been there for me over the years. Sometimes you didn't even know how much your friendship meant, but it was a gift. Friends have been a rare commodity for me and I cherish each and every one.

And most importantly to God, the one who held me in His arms and carried me when I had no strength to walk on my own. Who loved me when I didn't even believe He existed and was patiently guiding my life to awaken me to Himself.

Introduction

In reading over the original manuscript in preparation for editing, I became aware that the traumatic experiences related by the victim, needed to be written, so that healing could begin. But in order to make the book acceptable to public reading the graphic details must be eliminated, thereby making it a therapeutic book instead of a book that affects the emotions. In no way should this book be considered a book about illicit sex.

This book tells the story of a woman's too-long battle with the emotional and self-incriminating results of having experienced rape and incest in the innocence of childhood. If her story can help some entrapped mind, body, and soul, to grasp the faith that help is available, and healing is possible, that is the main and only goal of this book.

It is to alert and awaken parents to the possibility that this can happen to your child. That parents must be close to their children to realize when a child is carrying a guilt too great for their innocent little hearts and minds. And above and foremost, the child must know and experience the parent's all-encompassing love. As children feel and experience the love of a parent, it gives them a concept of the love of God. A child will be disobedient and rebellious at times, and will need discipline. The way parents react and handle the problem, will make a big difference on how the child thinks and feels about God.

An experience of a child whose innocence was stolen when he was exposed to vices by older children brings out a point that shows what love and discipline can accomplish.

The young innocent child was involved in something that some older boys had exposed him to. His parents had no idea what had happened, but they knew their child was not open and free as he had been. He actually avoided being near them. This was strange behavior as he was naturally a very loving child. They questioned him; nothing was wrong. And yet he kept his distance. They tried different avenues to unlock his innocent spirit. Through prayer and the wisdom of God they felt to apply discipline. It was then the chains of the incident were broken and he could unburden his guilt. As he felt the loving arms of his parents around him, he once again became the possessor of the happy carefree spirit of a child.

As much as we want to close our minds to the possibility that this can happen, we must admit it happens. And innocent children are often the victims.

This is the burden of this story.

L.T.

I

The bacon in the pan sizzled and popped, and slowly began to curl, sending a tantalizing aroma wafting through the house. It crept into the bedroom where Laurie was sleeping and gently tickled her nose. Sleepily she rubbed her eyes and twitched her nose; slowly the aroma awakened her and pulled her out of bed. She stumbled out down the hall to the bathroom, where she splashed water on her face. She looked up at the clock and a smile broke over her face. It was 4 o'clock in the morning and mother was frying bacon.

That could mean only one thing, they were going to the beach today! Quickly she dressed, putting her swimsuit on under her dress, and ran to the kitchen. She slid into her seat just as mother was putting the pancakes on the table. Her brothers Chad, Todd, and baby Joey were already there eating.

Laurie made short work of her breakfast and ran outside to find her dad. He was loading the fishing gear into the pickup, and checking the seine for holes. She helped him fold it up and tuck it in beside the fishing poles, they had to leave room for the ice chests as they would be needed to keep the fish fresh till they got home. Laurie ran to get them, there was just enough room beside the net. Then she ran back in the house to help mother finish packing the lunch. Finally they were all packed and ready to start. Anxiously Laurie watched the road for signs of approaching vehicles. At last they came, one after the other, Aunts and Uncles and cousins. They all had picnic baskets piled with good things to eat. It made Laurie's mouth water just thinking about all the yummy things in those baskets!

Every one was in high spirits, a friendly fight broke out among the boys, and the girls argued over which car to ride in. Laurie made sure she was in the second vehicle in line! Her dad's pickup would be first, but it was full already. Finally everyone was in and the heads were counted to make sure no one was missing. Then just as the sun began to peak over the horizon, they pulled out of the drive, one after the other, six vehicles in all. What a caravan they made! Laurie looking out the back window, could just make out the last car in the line.

It was a long drive to the beach, but everyone was so excited and the talking and teasing back and forth, made the miles pass quickly! And before long Laurie could see the water shimmering in the distance. Just a little farther and they were pulling onto the beach. They drove along on the sand until they found a spot that looked promising and unloaded the vehicles. The men set up a canopy for the women and babies, then took the net out and stretched it out on the sand. It was a long one, about 60 ft., with a four foot post at each end. After making sure it was not twisted or tangled, three men picked up the post on one end and waded into the water, another three men stayed on the beach with the other end. As the first three men got out into the deep water they began to circle back, making a big arch in the net. When they returned to shore they again spread the net on the sand, but this time it was full of fish. Everyone helped to pick them up and pack them in the ice chests. They the men repeated the whole process. Meanwhile the ladies fixed lunch under the canopy and Laurie and the cousins played on the beach and searched for seashells along the shore. When the men brought the net to shore everyone helped to pick up the fish. There were all sizes and kinds, some they threw back if they were too small. They found jelly fish and man-o-war, and sometimes they saw shark fins out in the water. After lunch Laurie and her cousins went swimming and wave riding. They swam out till their feet no longer touched the bottom, then let the waves carry them back to shore. Over and over till the motion of the waves seemed to become the pulse of their heart beat. It was late when the men decided to fold up the net.

The trip home was much quieter than the trip down had been. Everyone was exhausted, but it was an invigorating exhaustion!

That night when Laurie closed her eyes she could still feel the motion of the waves, and when she dreamed it was of the ocean, vast and beautiful, stretching away to the horizon but slowly changing till it surrounded her and she was standing on a sand bar with the tide getting higher and higher. It crept up on the sand bar making it smaller and smaller till it disappeared and still the water kept rising, the beach disappeared and there was no land in sight any where. Laurie awakened franticly swimming in the bed clothes, and for a moment she was unsure where she was. She lay awake then trying to calm her rapidly beating heart, and thinking, her life felt just like that dream, like she was desperately trying to keep her head above water but it was rising faster than she could swim. No help in sight and no land or place to rest as far as she could see. It made her feel claustrophobic not like her other dream. The peaceful one she dreamed sometimes when things happened that made her feel really sad. It wasn't a big thing Just an old country church standing at a crossroads, with a cross in front; everything around it perfectly peaceful. And in the back of her consciousness, the song, "Behold What Love," played over and over. It left her with a calm feeling whenever she thought of it, but what it meant, she did not know. Sometimes, she wondered if the words were some kind of message for her. There wasn't a doubt she needed one! Her Life was anything but peaceful. And to think someone would love her? hardly! She was only good for one thing; for other people to use and abuse. As she lay there in the dark thinking, the memories came in a rush. She remembered the first time her peaceful innocence had been shattered; she had been young, maybe five...

It was dark outside, and she hated the dark. Her dad and mom, and older sister, Heidi, were gone for the evening. Her older brothers were somewhere in the house. At the moment, she didn't know where, and that was fine. Alone in the house, she wandered around for a while, and then headed down the hall to the room she shared with Heidi. Just as she was passing her brother's room, Todd stepped out directly in front of her. Fear shot down her spine and twisted her insides. "Want to come play a game with me?" Laurie looked up at him. No, she did not want to, but the look on his face was not a question, it was a command; she had no choice. Todd was five years older than Laurie, and much bigger. She meekly followed him into his room and he quietly shut the door.

Laurie looked around franticly. Where was Chad? He was two years older than Todd and sometimes he protected her from him. When it was over she dressed with numb fingers, and as she was slipping out the door he said, "This is our little secret." Laurie stumbled to the bathroom. She felt dirty all over; she washed and washed; nothing she did made her feel clean again. Carefully avoiding the mirror, she opened the door and peaked out, no one was in sight. As quietly as possible she slipped into her parent's empty room, thankful her clothes were kept in her mother's dresser. Looking up she caught her reflection in the mirror.

Silently she screamed, "You are bad! You are dirty!" She ran to the dining room and grabbed a book. She pretended to read, but the words didn't make sense. She realized she was trying to hide, feeling sure that her guilt was written all over her face. When her parents returned it was bedtime. Quickly she got ready for bed, making sure to keep her face averted and not meet her mother's eyes. She would never look anyone in the eyes again, because, surely they would see how bad she was.

Slowly the days turned into a week, and then two. Apparently no one had noticed. Thankfully, yet lonelier than she had ever been in her life, Laurie learned to live with her guilt. She also learned to be aware of her surroundings at all times. She learned to stand at the edge of a room with her back to a wall. She learned to never turn a corner without trying to know what was around it. And as much as possible she avoided being near Todd. But, living in the same house made it difficult to always stay away from him, and one day it happened again.

. . . .

Stealthily she slipped out of the house and ran to find her bike. At least she could be alone for a while and wipe the guilt off her face.

She pedaled hard, trying to erase the memory. After awhile her legs began to protest, the muscles burned and felt like jelly. She slowed to a normal pace, and with an effort turned her mind off of the most recent experience.

She stayed outside as long as she could, but it was nearing supper time, and she was expected to help. It was her job to set the table for supper. At last she heard her mother calling, and with dragging feet she went inside. Laurie tried to forget what had happened, but her mind would not cooperate. The walls seemed to mock her, and she felt claustrophobic. Absently she placed the plates and cups on the table, and then slipped into a corner to wait for supper. She did not notice that the silverware was missing until her mother angrily demanded to know what she was doing, off playing, when her work wasn't finished. Guiltily she tried to slide the forks and spoons onto the table without being seen, but it was no good. Her mother saw, and for punishment Laurie was made to stand behind a chair and watch the rest of the family eat. She wasn't hungry anyway, her stomach hurt too much, but the imp inside her taunted her, "See you're bad. You can't even eat with the family. You might contaminate them."

Uncle John's had recently moved from another state, and now lived just a mile down the road. They had a son, Jack, just Laurie's age. Laurie and Jack hit it off from the start. He was a bright spot in her otherwise lonely world. They spent many hours riding bikes and playing in the barn on Laurie's dad's farm. In the summer they spent hours swimming in the stock tank that was Laurie's swimming pool. With Jack, she was just another child. She could forget for awhile that she was bad and dirty. However, sometimes Laurie would see Jack's mama watching her and she would remember. She felt like a liar. She was sure if Aunt Sue ever found out how bad she was, she would never let Jack play with her again. So she tried to stay out of sight as much as possible.

2

Jack and Laurie were now old enough to go to school. They would be attending a big public school in their nearby town. Laurie was frightened, but thought with Jack in her class she would be okay. The first day of school came, and Jack, Laurie, and several other children from their church group arrived at school. Laurie relaxed a little to see some familiar faces. Maybe it wouldn't be so bad.

Then school started and the children were assigned to their rooms. All the children from Laurie's group were assigned to the same room except her. She was sent upstairs to a separate room where she knew no one. Even their play times were different. Laurie knew she should not have expected to be in the same room with those she knew. She was bad, and the other children's parents wouldn't want her with their children, she was sure.

The first three months of school, she arrived crying every morning. Gradually she became accustomed to the strange place and people. She usually played alone at recess, never making friends, but she enjoyed learning. Laurie's second year of school started in a new school. The church group her parents attended built a private school over the summer and when school started, it was with a group of children that Laurie was acquainted with. Now she loved school! She loved to learn and she excelled at it. School became her refuge! Always she felt safe at school, and the children didn't seem to care that she was different, although she never felt like she fit in. She knew she was bad, but sometimes she could forget for awhile. She hated going home and would have lived at school if she could have. The church school they attended only had eight grades so Laurie and Todd were the only ones in school from their family. Often when she got home, there would be no one there except Todd.

That was the case one afternoon about half way through the school year. Laurie dashed into the house only to find it empty again; the rest of the family was in town. She ran to her room to change her clothes, but before she was finished, Todd called from his room. With leaden feet she walked down the hall. Todd stood in his bedroom doorway. Fear, like a white hot flash, exploded inside her head. . . .

The crunching of tires on the gravel driveway was heard. "Get to your room and then act like nothing happened," he hissed. Scared and trembling, she did as she was told. Coming out of her room into the hall she saw Todd step from his room, with a towel wrapped around his waist, as their mother came into the house. "Now we're caught," she thought. But her mother never seemed to think it strange that Todd was not dressed properly in the middle of the day.

Life fell into a routine; school during the day, and waiting for the evening to pass so she could go back to school the next morning. Laurie moved through each day as in a fog. She tried to be extra good to make up for the terrible things Todd made her do whenever they were alone. But no matter how good she was she never could erase the haunting guilt that hung over her like a cloud.

Laurie's schoolwork began to suffer; she could not seem to concentrate. One day she brought home a stack of papers with one paper carrying the dreaded grade of an F. Her mother became very stern. Laurie was made to understand clearly that every 'F' would be rewarded with a spanking. Nothing was said about the A's. So Laurie became more sneaky. When the papers were handed out, at the end of the week, she would quickly go through them and tear out any F's. On her way out of the classroom she would pass by the trashcan and push them way down in so no one would find them. The first time she did that she waited all evening for someone to find out, but no one noticed the torn page in her papers and each time she did it, it became easier to ignore the little voice telling her that it was wrong.

3

Every fall, the church Laurie's parents and Heidi belonged to, held a series of revival meetings. They would have two weeks of preaching every night when the entire families would gather. Then there would be meetings for members only. Laurie would be left home with Todd and Chad, as they were not members. One evening Laurie's parents left for church and the three of them were to clean up the supper table and wash the dishes. Chad washed the dishes and Todd dried, while Laurie cleaned the table. Laurie was happy. Chad was there, so there was no need to worry. Her brothers teased and talked with each other and her; it would be a good evening. But just as the last dishes were being put away the teasing changed. Todd started talking very sweetly to her, it made Laurie extremely fearful and uncomfortable! There was only one reason he ever talked like that to her. Just as the last dish was being put away, he asked if she would like to see some magic.

Laurie was not expecting that, maybe he really was just trying to be nice. Telling her to watch their hands, both boys walked out of the kitchen onto the porch with their hands held above their heads, then turned and faced Laurie. Both were standing there with their jeans unzipped and exposing themselves. Laurie was shocked! Todd had done this kind of thing many times, but never when Chad was around. Repeatedly they did it, trying to make her guess how they accomplished

11

the "magic." Finally, Chad tired of it and said he was going to take a shower.

Laurie remained where she was sitting on a chair hoping Todd would leave also, but he didn't. Shortly Chad called to her from the bathroom and with dragging feet, she went to see what he wanted. She was afraid she knew, but hoped she was wrong. She stood outside the bathroom door and waited to see what he would do. Finally he said, "Oh, nothing." Thankfully, she walked back out to the dining room, glad that she could still trust Chad. However, the evening was not yet over. Todd was waiting for her with his jeans still unzipped. She stopped on the other side of the room from him, hoping he would not molest her again. But he said, "Come here."

Laurie was sickened. He had never made her touch him before. She felt ill and nausea hit her. Laurie ran to the washroom and turned the water on, scrubbing and scrubbing with soap, trying to wash away the repulsiveness of the experience. There was a sharp rap on the door. Laurie jumped as though she had been shot, fear surged through her. Then her mother's voice demanded, "What are you doing in there? Turn that water off and quit playing."

Laurie turned off the water, and then with an effort, she wiped any emotions off her face. She would close the door of her mind on this evening and never open it again.

That night Laurie dreamed. In her dream, she saw a church with a steeple, all painted white. The grass around it was a deep lush green. To Laurie, it seemed as though she was standing on the steps looking out. In front of her, she could see two roads meeting directly in front of the church. They seemed to be covered with deep sand, and right in the center where they met there stood a cross. Music seemed to be coming from somewhere, maybe from the church, and the song it was singing was an old one Laurie had heard many times in church. "Behold what love, yes, love divine the Father showed to thee; . . . Such love cannot be fathomed tis like the boundless sea. His broken heart so wounded is bleeding now for thee." The dream made her feel peaceful. In the morning when she awoke, she lay in bed for a little while trying to bring back the dream just the way it had been. She didn't want to forget it.

Later as she sat at the breakfast table trying to eat, she looked up and caught Todd staring at her.

Her stomach clenched as the memory of last night flooded over her. She felt like she was going to be sick again. One look at her mother and she swallowed hard, it would never do to be sick here, her mom would be angry!

Laurie watched the clock hands move slowly around to eight o'clock. Never had they moved so slowly! Finally the school bus arrived. Thankfully, she ran to the vehicle and climbed in. Usually Laurie felt like she was locked in a box with just a barred window through which she watched the rest of the world. But at school she could come out, be someone else and watch the other children play, sometimes even joining in. She still had that stupid little Laurie person dragging around behind her, but she could forget her for a while.

One day the teacher read a story about a girl named Laurie, but her friends all called her Aurie. So Laurie became Aurie when she was out of the box. She told the children at school to call her that, and she even signed her papers that way, until the teacher saw it. The teacher was not impressed. She told Laurie she must use her own name. Aurie felt sorry for the little box girl, but she didn't let it bother her too much. So Aurie went to school, won the spelling bee, and was at the head of the math class. Aurie made friends with the other girls, skipped rope the longest, and jumped the highest. However, the other girls teased Laurie because her dresses didn't have puffed sleeves and circle skirts. Laurie wore white socks while the other girls wore colored ones. And Laurie cheated in class and was caught and had to stay in and write sentences. And when all the other girls got together for a sleep over Laurie's mom would not let her go.

4

aurie loved anything outdoors and after much coaxing, she talked her dad into letting her have a calf to raise. She would get up early every morning to feed her calf, and before long she was given the job of feeding all the calves. She didn't care, she loved the early morning with the world all fresh and dew-washed.

For a little while each morning she was happy and it seemed to Laurie, as though life was worth living after all. If she could only erase the memories, life would be good again. However, she couldn't, and every time she was close to Todd, she felt like she couldn't breathe. Sometimes if she happened to catch him looking at her, it seemed as if he was accusing her.

Finally she could stand it no longer. With her heart pounding, she wrote a little note and put in her mother's Sunday school book. Then she waited anxiously for her to find it. On Saturday morning her mother called her to her room and asked her what it meant. Tremblingly she tried to explain, but words failed her. Finally, Laurie's mother seemed to understand, and Laurie felt for a moment as though a great weight had been lifted from her shoulders. Then her mother asked if she was sure she wasn't making things up, to get Todd in trouble. Laurie was stunned; "No! she would never make something like that up!" Her mother was not convinced, she thought it was probably Laurie's fault, she must have tempted him. She proceeded to give Laurie a lecture about the way a girls actions can tempt a boy.

Laurie understood very little of it. She was only eight years old. However, she did understand it was her fault, and that her mother was very displeased with her. The rest of the day was miserable for Laurie. She wished she would not have told her mother anything, because it didn't help. In fact, she felt worse, as her mother kept looking at her accusingly. Laurie thought the day would never end, but eventually it did. She slept fitfully that night; it seemed as though she had lost something that day that left her unsettled. Finally, towards morning, she fell into a deeper sleep and then she dreamed. As before, the setting was so peaceful, the white church with its steeple against a blue, blue sky, and lush green grass, and in the center of the crossroads, a cross pointing to heaven. The singing again seemed to be coming from the church, but it surrounded the entire scene and seemed to fill Laurie's whole being. She could distinctly hear the words, "Behold what love, yes love divine the Father showed to thee, . . . His broken heart so wounded, is bleeding now for thee." She would have liked to just keep sleeping and never wake up, but long before she was ready her mother was calling her and as she slowly awakened, the peaceful feeling faded away.

Suddenly she remembered yesterday, and fear flooded her. "What if mom told dad what I told her? I'll probably get a spanking." Laurie was afraid of her dad when her mom was around. When she was alone with him she felt loved and secure, but she knew if mom told him she needed a spanking she would get it. And his spankings hurt! She had counted one time when one of the boys was whipped. They got forty-two licks. She knew if he found out what she had done, she was in trouble.

With trembling fingers, she dressed and went to the kitchen to help with breakfast. Her dad and brothers were not in from the barn yet, and as she set the table, she felt as though her fear would choke her. Finally when she felt she could not stand another minute, they came in with the boys arguing over who got to use the washroom first. Her dad didn't even look at her. Relief washed over her, so intense that she felt weak. Apparently her mom hadn't told him. But she had been looking at Laurie with that look, that Laurie understood to mean, "I found you out! I know how bad you are now, and now you are going to get it."

All morning while they were eating breakfast and during family devotions and while they were washing dishes, Laurie waited for the blow to fall. But it never did. Then as she was brushing her teeth, Todd came to the bathroom and said, "I'm sorry for all that stuff." He left as though he didn't want to be in the same room with her. Laurie didn't care, she didn't want to be in the same room with him, either. She wondered if he really meant what he said. She supposed time would tell, but now at least she knew her mother must have told her dad. She couldn't figure out why she had been let off without a whipping. Her dad never acted as if anything had happened, except it seemed he avoided being near her. Laurie wasn't sure; it could be she just imagined it. But sometimes it seemed as though his eyes said, "I can't stand you; you're dirty and bad." So Laurie stayed away from him as much as possible.

It seemed to Laurie that all she did these days was stay away from people. She had been going to church with her family since she was born, and knew what the Bible said about God loving every one the same, and the dream always made her feel loved for as long as it lasted. But with wakefulness came the horrible realization that she was not a part of the human race. She didn't know what she was, just that she lived in a different zone from the rest of the world. It seemed to Laurie that there was an invisible line where her world of darkness was divided from the real world.

. . . .

Laurie's parents built a new house and they were moving into it just before school let out for the summer. Aurie was allowed to stay home moving day. She felt very important. All day she carried boxes and bags and helped pack and unpack. When school was over Jack came over, too, as Uncle John's were helping with the moving. Then Aurie and Jack went outside and played. What fun they had; Aurie wished this day would never end. It seemed like everyone was in a festive mood. However, eventually most of the helpers went home.

One of Laurie's great Aunt's brought supper over and they all sat around their new table in the new kitchen and ate chili. After supper, Laurie's mom wanted to finish putting up the curtains in the bedroom, and everyone went to offer advice. Quietly Aurie slipped back to the kitchen, cleared the table, and washed up all the dishes. She was almost finished when Aunt Sally came bustling out to do the dishes. Her mouth dropped open in astonishment. Then she did something Laurie hadn't counted on; she hugged her, and praised her profusely. Laurie was embarrassed, she couldn't remember anyone ever praising her for anything before. She decided she didn't like it, it made her uncomfortable. It was never good to have attention focused on her, someone might find out how bad she really was!

Laurie liked their new house, it was big and open and Laurie's bedroom was at the opposite end from her brothers. She no longer had to pass their bedroom to get to her own. Laurie's dad built a new swing set for her and her little brother, Joey. She spent hours soaring into the sky. When she was up there she pretended she was soaring like a bird. It almost seemed like she could just fly away and never return. She dreamed about the places she would go and it was great fun to imagine the conversations she would have. In her dream world, she was loved and protected and she always belonged.

5

Laurie's dad sometimes hooked up his gooseneck trailer and went up north to buy hay for his cows. The day he took Laurie with him was the best day of her life! They left early, before it was even light. It was so cozy in the pickup with the dash lights casting a warm glow on the seat cover, that Aurie curled up against the seat back and fell asleep. It was light when she awakened. They stopped at a little station and Aurie could pick anything she wanted to eat for her breakfast snack. What fun! Later, after they had loaded their hay, her dad said they would stop at a café or the sale barn for dinner, but it might be four o'clock.

It was long after dark when they returned home. It had definitely been a wonderful "Aurie" day!

. . . .

Summer was in full swing; long, hot days with nothing to do. Oh, there were the usual chores, like dishes and dusting, and sweeping the porch, but then there were hours when Laurie could ride her bike or play with her kittens. Sometimes Aunt Sue brought over Jack and his little brother, Jerry, and they would swim in the big round stock tank Laurie's dad had bought for her. Those were good times, "Aurie" times. Sometimes Aurie's dad would let her ride with him in the field when he was discing. Then came the day he taught her to drive the tractor.

She was sure that was the best day of her life! Later as she got older she learned to disc and plant. And daddy said she could plant straighter rows than her brothers could.

Summer Sunday afternoons were times for naps and reading, and occasionally, if they asked just right, the children would be allowed to bring a friend home from church. So it happened one Sunday that Todd brought his friend, Richard, home for dinner. Laurie liked Richard, and, as he was Todd's best friend, she had become accustomed to having him around. After dinner and dishes, Laurie's parents went to take their usual nap. Her older brother and sister left for a youth gathering, and Todd and Richard went outside with the intention of exploring the swollen creek behind the house. Laurie, who had been forbidden to go near the creek without an older person, saw her chance, and begged to be included. Reluctantly the boys told her she could come. It was a short walk to the creek which ran behind the house, and normally it was just a trickle, but a heavy rain the night before had filled it to overflowing. It was intriguing to watch.

They wandered around for a while throwing in sticks and watching them swirl away, but soon they tired of it, and returned to the house. Laurie ran ahead, and was on the swing, slowly swinging when they got there. Coming over to where she was, Todd told her that she owed them something for taking her with them. She wondered what they wanted, but was not too concerned. After all Todd had told her he was sorry. Also, he had been baptized, and was now a church member. Besides Richard was there. Todd told her to follow them, and when they reached the bedroom her brothers shared, she hesitantly followed them in. Quietly shutting the door Todd asked her if she remembered their game. Numbly she nodded. "We took you with us, now you owe us. If you don't behave I'll tell mom you went to the creek." Whatever happened, Laurie knew her mom would never believe her ahead of Todd. She would be accused of lying and trying to get him in trouble.

Later shocked and trembling from the terrible experience with the boys, Laurie stumbled to her room and locked the door behind her. Catching sight of herself in the mirror, she silently screamed, "I hate you! You're stupid and ugly!" She bounced around the room unable to stand herself, yet unable to get away from herself. She wished she could crawl into a deep dark hole and disappear forever. If she could just quit breathing.

She tried holding her breath, and was starting to feel faint when she heard her mother calling her to help with supper. She tried to ignore her, but she called again, more insistent, and Laurie knew she had better go. Keeping her head down and avoiding her mother as much as possible, she set the table and ran back to her room. Her mother thought she was just being lazy, and told her she better straighten up and quit being such a grouch. "I hate you," she silently screamed at her. Telling her mother she wasn't hungry, she remained in her room until the family was ready to leave for the evening church service. Waiting until the last minute, she walked from her room to the vehicle without speaking to anyone.

All evening Laurie stayed by herself. She stood in a corner behind a group of ladies, and was nearly invisible. She shut her mind to the memories, but the dirty feeling remained. She longed for someone to talk to, but there was no one she trusted. And no one noticed the pain on her face. The dream came again that night, and as before, it left her with a comfort she didn't understand. There had been other dreams, that were unforgettable, but the one with the cross and the church came again and again. Laurie clung to it at times like this, when it felt like the bottom had fallen out of her world.

Time moved on, but Laurie couldn't. School was her only refuge, and it wouldn't start for another month. What was she to do with herself in the meantime? Staying out of the house was not an option, although she tried. It made her mom angry. She accused Laurie of trying to get out of work, and so Laurie would hurry through her chores and hang around for a few minutes. If her mom didn't say anything she would slip outside. She could usually find her dad behind the barn working on machinery. She liked to help him, and he seemed to appreciate her help. Laurie was careful not to mention the house or her mother, because he would wonder what she was doing outside and send her in to help her mom. If she kept quiet, he wouldn't think about it.

The first time he went to try out the combine she was riding in the cab. There was a fascination to watching that big reel gobble up the beans.

Quietly Laurie watched and took it all in. She soon knew which levers lowered the head or turned on the reel. She watched as he engaged the spout to unload into the gravity wagon. She didn't talk or ask questions, there was no need. Sometimes her dad would explain something, but mostly they rode in companionable silence. If the machine plugged she was right in there with him, pulling the vines out. Sometimes she crawled right inside, as she could fit better than her dad.

At last her chance came. Her dad had to run to the farm to empty the gravity wagon and she was allowed to run the combine alone. Laurie was thrilled! She had driven it for a while a few times, but always her dad had been right there. Now she was alone! There couldn't have been a more careful driver. She would sooner die than make a mistake. When her dad returned, he said he couldn't have done a better job. Laurie learned to drive the tractor, too. Then she would haul the wagons to the farm and unload them into the bin. Soon she was outside more than she was in. Her dad made her feel like she was a necessary part of the farm work and she loved it. Indoors she could never work fast enough or good enough for her mom. No matter how hard she tried her mother always disapproved of her efforts.

So Laurie stayed outside more and more. Of course, she always had to face her mother's disapproving looks when she went in, but if she stayed out of her way until her dad came in, her mom wouldn't say anything in front of him. So Laurie spent her days driving tractor. She found out that she could keep her mind busy with her tasks and then she didn't think about the other side of her life. She was almost happy when she was all by herself. When school started again Laurie was not anxious to go after all; it meant she would miss out on the harvesting. It was good to get back to the familiar schedule, though, and it turned out that she was needed to drive tractor when she got home from school.

So summer turned to fall and fall to winter, and Laurie was kept so busy she didn't have to time to think. When the harvesting was over and the long winter evenings began, Laurie found that the sharp edge of shame had dulled with the passage of time. It still haunted her, but she had learned that keeping her mind totally occupied, kept her from thinking. And how better to do that when outside with the animals, or inside reading? So when there was no longer anything to keep her busy around the farm, she would study the encyclopedias or the dictionary. Sometimes she would put puzzles together; the hard ones, so her mind was busy. On the nice days when she could be outside, she would ride her bike by the hour.

She was now old enough that she was allowed to ride on the road. Laurie's dad farmed the land on both sides of the road for almost a half mile. Laurie would ride to the very edge of the fields, then turn around and coast back home. Repeatedly she rode up the road and back, pretending someone was watching and she didn't dare make a mistake. She was Aurie, and Aurie didn't make mistakes anyway. If she did, she would reprimand Laurie severely and tell her to go back home. These long rides alone kept her from going insane. She felt almost normal. Almost happy. As soon as she returned to the yard, reality returned. She felt safe with her bike and the wide open road. Until one day . . .

. . . .

Todd would sometimes come up behind her in the pickup, driving so close to the shoulder that she would have to ride into the ditch to let him pass. The ditches were steep so she stopped and waited for him to pass. This day, instead of driving on, he got out and came over to her. Kneeling down on the road he pretended to check her bike chain, then while still kneeling there with her straddling her bike, he ran his hand up her leg. Laurie went still as a statue, her head started spinning, she could hardly breathe. Laurie didn't know how long she stayed standing there. When he stood up and walked back to the pickup she was not surprised when he told her to meet him in the barn.

Slowly she pedaled back home hoping maybe he'd be busy by the time she got there, and she could sneak into the house. But as soon as she started up the drive she could see him standing there waiting for her. As a snake hypnotizes its victims, so Laurie was paralyzed with fear. Escape seemed impossible, and once again she became a victim to her brother's demands.

Leaving the barn she wanted to run and run and never look back.

Instead, she walked slowly to the house. Slowly she opened the door. She didn't want to be seen until she had time to close her mind on the whole ugly happening. She quietly stepped into the house, being careful not to let the door make a squeak. Placing her feet softly, and without making a sound, she managed to slip past the kitchen where her mother was working. The moment she felt safe, she bolted for her bedroom, but her mother must have heard the door. Laurie heard her full name in a stern tone. She was caught. She made her face blank as she was turning around and when she faced her mother, she plastered a smile on.

Her mother became very upset, demanding to know what she had been doing that she had to sneak around. Laurie looked at her mother's feet and thought how she hated the slippers she always wore. Suddenly Laurie realized her mother was no longer talking and she was expected to answer. But she didn't have an answer; she hadn't been listening. Her mom really became upset then, saying something about if she wasn't doing anything wrong she wouldn't have to sneak around. Laurie kept an apologetic look on her face, and pretended to listen. She knew that her mother thought she was wicked. She figured it was true, look what had just happened?

Laurie really did try to do everything she was supposed to do. But she just couldn't seem to do enough to erase the bad. If there was a God, as she had been told, then she was sure He hated her. It would not be possible to love someone as bad as she was. Laurie didn't know why she had been born. She wondered if maybe she was adopted. She had read stories about adopted children and some were bad, just like her. She had also noticed that Jack was never bad and she knew he was not adopted. Therefore, she must be, and no one liked adopted children.

6

Jack and Laurie were still friends but they had begun to grow apart. Jack was also learning to drive tractor and help Uncle John on their farm, and he didn't especially appreciate a girl competing with him. Jack had made friends with many of the boys from church and didn't really need any "girl" friends. Laurie kept herself apart. Oh, she played with the other girls, but she never really made friends. So when it was announced at the supper table one night that Uncle Ron's were returning to the states from their mission post, Laurie's ears perked up. Uncle Ronnie's had a girl just a few months older than Laurie. Soon the news came that, not only were Uncle Ronnie's coming home, they were coming to live just a few miles from Laurie's family. Laurie didn't really know Maggie, but she did remember playing with her at their grandma's house.

Grandma lived close to Uncle Ronnie's old home so Laurie didn't see her often, either, as it was a twelve hour drive to her house. Laurie's dad found a farm for Uncle Ronnie's to buy, the deal was made, and plans were made for Laurie's parents to help them move. The trip was planned for the Christmas holidays so they could all spend Christmas with Grandma. Laurie was so excited she could hardly wait. Grandma lived where there was snow in the winter, and Laurie couldn't remember ever seeing snow. There was a festive feeling in the air. Laurie's mother was buying all kinds of presents for Uncle Ronnie's family. Candy, toys, and dishes; there was a whole suitcase full. They had been in the mission for seven years so they needed lots of stuff to set up housekeeping in the States again.

Laurie caught the spirit, too. She picked out a little glass candy dish for Maggie, and talked her mother into buying coloring books and colors, for Maggie's little sister and brother. It was exciting! Laurie's mom told her they would not be getting any gifts that year as they were giving to Uncle Ronnie's instead. She didn't really care, it was such fun imagining their faces as they opened the packages.

At last, the long awaited day arrived. Laurie's mother woke her up while it was still dark. Sleepily she struggled into her clothes. The rest of the family, except Joey, was sitting at the table when she finally appeared. Silently they ate breakfast. Laurie didn't want to eat, she was too tired, but her mother insisted she eat something. They didn't plan to eat dinner for a long time. By the time the sun came up, they had been driving for several hours. Laurie thought it was the longest day she had ever lived through. It was interesting watching the scenery change and seeing all the little towns, but by the time they finally reached their destination, Laurie thought she never wanted to see a road again! Towards evening Daddy was finally turning into the driveway and there was Uncle Ronnie's family waiting for them. It had been decided they would all have supper together at Uncle Joe and Aunt Tina's.

Uncle Joe's had a big two-story house with lots of bedrooms. Uncle Ronnie's were staying with them until they moved. The evening passed as in a dream for Laurie. She and Maggie had such fun getting acquainted. They hit it off right away, and had no trouble finding plenty to talk about. They played outside for a long time and when they were finally called in to get ready for bed they were fast friends. They were put in a bedroom upstairs all by themselves. They felt so big!

They sat on the bed and talked and giggled until Laurie thought she would fall asleep sitting up. Then they turned out the light and crawled under the covers. Laurie was almost asleep, but Maggie was still talking. She wondered if Laurie wanted to play a new game she had learned. Laurie was so tired she just wanted to sleep, but she didn't want to make Maggie upset, either. So she agreed, not knowing what Maggie was up to. A white hot flash exploded inside Laurie's head when she discovered what Maggie meant. She felt like she had been slapped hard across the face. Not willing to lose a friend, Laura played the game, but something inside her died.

Long after Maggie had fallen asleep Laurie lay awake. Her chest hurt, she wanted to cry, but it had been a habit for so long to not give in to tears, that she couldn't. The trip was ruined for Laurie. She let her mother think she was just worn out from playing so hard, but really, she didn't want to be alone with Maggie. She was glad when it was time to go home. Laurie's mother was upset with her. She told her she had no right to be so stuck up, and it was her responsibility to make sure Maggie was not left out at school. Laurie did what she had to, to keep peace, but no more.

The first year or so that Uncle Ronnie's were there, it seemed to Laurie that they were together all the time. Often Maggie would want Laurie to spend the night with her. Laurie tried to get out of it, but her mother made her go because she thought Laurie was being snooty. Oh, if only she could tell her mother why she didn't want to go! But she could not. Laurie hated herself. She knew it was her fault; she was bad.

The girls grew farther and farther apart. And Laurie's mother kept trying to push them back together. She told Laurie it was the devil in her that made her act as if she thought she was better than Maggie. Laurie knew better than that. She knew that *she* was bad. If she would have stopped to think about it she would have thought it unfair. She had been bad before she even had a chance to make a choice. Apparently, she had been created bad. She hated herself; she wanted to be like other girls. If she thought about the things she had done it made her curl into a ball and try to hide from everyone. So she didn't think. She made her mind blank and just lived automatically. Her teachers and the other girls at school thought she was stupid. Her mom thought she was stubborn and lazy. Laurie tuned them all out. On the rare occasion she did something right, she was ashamed at the attention she got. It was not really meant for her, of this she was positive. She tried to make sure she never did anything wrong, but did not want to be too outstandingly good, either. That way she never had attention focused on her.

7

There was stress at home now, more than ever. Todd was becoming very rebellious. Hardly a day went by without a confrontation. He was caught with magazines that were sinful, and ordered to destroy them. It made him very angry. Finally, he decided it was enough. He went to town, got a job, and moved out. Laurie was secretly glad! She had hated living in the same house with him. It was much more peaceful with him gone.

Laurie went to church with her parents every Sunday. Her school was a church school, and every summer she attended Bible School. She was very well acquainted with the Bible, and knew what it said about sin. It was a sin to ever disagree with those older than she. And she must never disobey! Hatred for sure was a sin. And she knew her heart was full of hate. She hated herself the most. But also her mother and Todd. Sometimes she felt like she hated the whole world.

Laurie's heart became more and more heavy. Revivals came again, and every night Laurie sat and listened. In the past, she had been able to close the part of her mind where the memories were hidden, but this time the door kept popping open. Finally towards the end of the revivals there was a particularly strong sermon about hell, and then the song was sung, "Just as I Am." Laurie was shaking so badly she could not even sing. After the benediction an older girl that was sitting by her asked her if she was afraid; she told her, "yes." The girl told her to go home, pray about it, and tell Jesus she was afraid. This she did. As she was kneeling beside her bed, it seemed to her that there was a light in the distance. She longed to move toward it, but the darkness that surrounded her was so heavy it seemed to follow her.

She stayed there on her knees for a long time, not really praying, but with her heart straining toward that light. She lost track of time, but at last the darkness seemed to recede and she felt like she was standing in the outer edges of the circle of light. There was lightness about her, and she felt for the first time as if she could walk with her head up like others. Maybe this was what was considered being born again. Some time later, she was visiting with the minister and told him about her feeling. He agreed she must have been converted. So she was baptized, along with a group of her classmates. Now she was also a church member, but more importantly, she seemed to feel the arms of Jesus around her.

That was a new sensation. To feel like she was special to someone! She didn't know how to act, it made her euphoric! Also, for once, she had done something her mother approved of.

Laurie was in her last year of school and it was an eventful one. All three of her older siblings got married with in a few months of each other. Chad got married first. He had left the church and married a girl from town. She was pregnant when they got married, and their son was born about 2 months later. Todd married a girl from town, and they also had a child shortly. Heidi married and moved fourteen hundred miles away. After graduation Laurie took over the babysitting job, Heidi had been doing. She also baby-sat her niece and nephew frequently. Life was full and good! Chad's wife, "Rachel," became a very close friend. Two of her grandmothers had raised her until the age of eight. Then she was pushed from one relative to the other until she met Chad. She, too, knew abuse and loneliness, which seemed to create a special bond between her and Laurie. For the first time in her life, Laurie felt accepted for herself. She didn't have to pretend to be something she wasn't.

They spent hours together, talking and laughing and playing with the baby. Early fall came and one of Laurie's cousins was expecting a baby, and had to be on total bed rest. They asked Laurie to come and help them. She spent four weeks living with them, caring for their one child, and doing all the household chores. One evening after supper, Laurie took the food scraps out to throw over the fence. The hired man happened to be out fixing fence and he began talking to her. They talked for a long time and it was getting dark when Laurie went in, but she had made another friend.

As time went on, Raymond became the security she had never had. His father had left the family when Raymond was eleven, and he had become the man of the house over night. He also understood loneliness and insecurity. Laurie found she could tell him anything, and he always believed her. Sometimes when she was really upset he would just listen while she yelled, or cried, or whatever. When she was all done he just asked, "Feel better now?" And she usually did. He noticed when she was feeling down by the look on her face. He would take her aside and make her share what was troubling her. And she did the same for him. People began noticing they were always together and started talking. It made Laurie upset, but she wasn't about to give up her friendship. They started sneaking their times together. Nothing was going to break up their friendship!

Raymond worked for Laurie's dad one summer, and often he would work late in the fields. After everyone was in bed he would come scratch on Laurie's screen, then they would sit and talk. Many times, he had been witness to the degrading comments from her mother, and was concerned about Laurie's state of mind. More than once, he talked her out of taking her own life. He was her rock, even after he moved to another state. Laurie would get a roll of quarters from the bank, and call him from a gas station pay phone. He always had time to talk to her no matter what. And even when they didn't talk for months, she always knew he was there if she needed him.

Laurie's first summer out of school, she spent working for Mark and Marla. Marla was Laurie's cousin, and they owned a truck garden. Laurie loved working there, being away from home, working outside, working with other people. However, most of all she loved working with Mark's family!! They all worked together picking beans, and cucumbers, filling orders for produce and stocking the roadside stand. Laurie loved all of it. Something about Mark's place and family made her feel peaceful, like the dream. They were another refuge in her otherwise stormy world. The next two summers were spent working there, also. Mark was a minister and he seemed to truly care. Gradually Laurie began to trust him. Not enough to tell him her "secret" yet, but enough to listen when he talked to her about life. She was having a hard time living the way she knew she was supposed to according to the church. She saw no reason to pretend to be something she wasn't and she sure wasn't "good" or "righteous"!

As for being a Christian, she didn't want to be one if her mom was! However, after working with Mark's for three summers and spending lots of time observing their family, she decided maybe there was more to it than she had believed. For some reason, that she couldn't understand, Mark's accepted her just like she was. Even when she tried to be unlikable, they still treated her with love.

So it happened that the next time revivals came around, and Mark asked her to visit with the visiting ministers, she agreed, under the condition that he would be in the visit. She was seventeen, and it seemed like her "secret" was getting bigger all the time. Laurie decided it was time to test Mark and see if he would believe her. Very carefully, she introduced the subject, careful to give only the barest details. She was trying the waters to see if they would overflow. Silence, complete silence. She looked up expecting to see disbelief and revulsion. Instead, she saw belief, and, — was that pity? Laurie didn't want pity, just someone to believe her and still befriend her, even when they knew how bad she was.

Laurie had become accustomed to wearing dark glasses to hide her eyes, and usually Mark made her take them off when he was talking to her. He said he "wanted to see what she was thinking." This time she was very glad she had them on because her eyes started watering. It must have been something in the air because *"she didn't cry!"* After a few minutes of silence she risked another look at Mark, and was immediately sorry she had. That was "Love" she saw in his eyes. She was sure of it! It made her uncomfortable. She didn't know how to act. She was used to disapproval and disgust, and this was something she didn't understand. Gently, then, the ministers began to ask questions, and never did they make her feel like she was lying or stupid. When she left Mark's that day she felt like a weight had been lifted from her shoulders, but another one had taken its place. Love hurt! She would not make herself that vulnerable again. As a result of that visit she was asked to go away for awhile. Laurie chose to go to Uncle Steve's in Canada.

8

She didn't know Uncle Steve's real well, but they had recently visited and Uncle Steve had gone out of his way to speak to Laurie all by herself. She nearly worshipped him! Plans were made, ticket bought, and shortly Laurie was on her way to Ontario.

She would spend eight months there. Eight months unlike any she had previously experienced. And one night Uncle Steve sat Laurie down, after the rest of the family was in bed, and dragged from her the key to the Pandora's box with all the past she kept hidden inside. Laurie let him peak just a little, then carefully closed and locked the lid again. But it no longer closed tightly. It seemed as though the opening of the box had warped the lid a little, the contents kept wanting to walk out. Laurie tried to push them back in, but they didn't want to stay. So she stayed up, after everyone was in bed, and wrote a letter revealing the top layer of the contents in the box. She folded it carefully, wrote Uncle Steve's name on the outside, and left it lying on the table.

Several days went by in which Laurie called herself all kinds of a fool. Uncle Steve had not said one word about the letter. She wished she could take it back. She was sure Uncle Steve hated her; she'd be sent home; she was dirty and evil, and he wouldn't want her around his children! Then one night while she was sitting at the table writing in her diary, Uncle Steve came into the kitchen. He put his arms around

Laurie and held her. When he let go there were tears in his eyes. They talked then and for a little while, Laurie felt like someone cared.

But life moved on, and it wasn't long until she realized, that may have only been an illusion, an emotion of the moment, a figment of her imagination. The reality was, she was different, bad, dirty, and unlovable. So the time came for her to go home. Laurie would have liked to stay, but she knew she didn't belong there, and already she felt guilty for imposing on good people for so long.

After she got back home, one night she dreamed she met Uncle Steve's daughter. She asked how they were doing, and the daughter told her it was time she had gone home, because Aunt Christie had been down in bed ever since Laurie left; she was so stressed out from having Laurie there. The dream was so real she believed it, and another layer of guilt was added to her load. Laurie knew she should never have dragged Uncle Steve's into her mire. She was like a mouse. They have no bladder, so every where they go, they leave a disgusting trail. At least at home her trail wasn't contaminating innocent victims.

. . . .

She had been gone long enough that it took awhile to get reconnected. Two weeks after she returned, on a Friday afternoon, Laurie put the little girl she was babysitting in the car, and left to pick up Joey from school. About half way to school was a hill, and just beyond that, a curve with another highway joining right on the curve. As Laurie topped the hill, there was a cloud of dust just settling, and right where the two roads met, a horrific jumble of twisted metal. As she approached, she recognized the back end of one of the vehicles. Shaking and with pounding heart, she pulled off the road. As she put the car in park, her former eighth grade teacher appeared outside her window. As she opened her door, he shook his head. He said, "It's Penney and she's out." He wouldn't let Laurie go over to the car. He had been up to the car already and she wasn't responding. He told Laurie she better go on. The grim look on his face told her it was bad.

Penney was taken by ambulance to the next city, some fifty miles away. She never regained consciousness and passed away during the early morning hours. Laurie's heart ached, but she didn't cry. She wished she could, and then felt guilty for wishing it. She knew she had no right to hurt. She had been gone for eight months, and had barely been with Penney since she returned. There were others who were much closer to her than Laurie. So she didn't cry.

During the days leading up to the funeral, she tried to be supportive of Penney's family and other close friends, but not intrude in their grief. It was a hard road to walk, hiding her own grief to not take attention away from others. Laurie had been close friends with the whole family, before she left for Canada, and they seemed to want her there to lean on. She did her best, and after the funeral she was nearly collapsing. She slipped away and went home, where her dad was very happy to see her. He had field work that needed doing, and Laurie gladly climbed on the tractor and headed to the field. It was a beautiful autumn day and as she drove from one end of the field to the other, she allowed herself to grieve. She didn't cry; almost she wished she could. But at least she worked through the crushing pain that had been building inside. The next day she went, alone, to look at the car.

Laurie began working for Uncle John. He owned a furniture refinishing business and needed help. Uncle John told her before she started that he couldn't pay much. She took the job anyway. She loved it. Uncle John was a fun loving person, and he enjoyed teasing her. Aunt Sue was a happy, loving person and a terrific cook. Laurie sometimes imagined Uncle John's were her family. The money she did get was only a bonus. Her real wages was the acceptance she felt. She worked for Uncle John's for almost a year.

9

Laura's sister, Heidi, was having surgery and needed help, so she flew out to help. After the surgery and recuperation, it was harvest time and Laurie had been planning to stay for harvest, but the school board asked her to work at school three days a week. She also worked at the local bakery part time. The bakery manager, Sherry, was a single girl, some years her senior, but despite the age difference they became very good friends.

Sherry lived alone in a big, old, two story house. Laurie spent hours there. They grilled hamburgers on the porch, laid out in the sun, installed mud flaps on Sherrie's car; Laurie held the screws. And when it was too cold for outdoor activities, they made popcorn and stood over the heat vent, talking. They went shopping together, and out to eat, and went to Canada for a wedding. Then as winter was waning, Sherry decided to visit her parents for Easter. She asked Laurie to go with her.

It was an eight hour drive, and they both had to work Good Friday evening, so Laurie made sure her suitcase was packed, and after work she went home for a quick change, and soon they were on their way. It was late when they started and they were both tired, so to help themselves stay awake, they took along a book, Vinegar Boy, and Laurie read aloud. The book was about Jesus crucifixion, and the next day being Easter, they wanted to finish it. So when they stopped for the night, Sherry took over reading the last few chapters. It was after midnight when they pulled into the hotel, and everything was quiet. They were careful to be quiet until they reached their room. They showered, put on night shirts, and curled up with pillows to finish reading. It felt good to relax, and Sherry was a good reader. They were almost finished when they heard a noise that drew their attention. They listened a bit, but didn't hear anything, so joking about it being a little man in the corner, they continued reading. The noise came again, this time louder and right outside their window. They both ran to the window and looked out. Sherry's car, parked right below their second story window, was being broken into.

The night clerk at the front desk didn't even ask questions. He just grabbed something out of his desk drawer and ran outside. He stopped the car as it was pulling out. A radar detector had been stolen from Sherry's car, and the police found it, among other things, in the escape vehicle. When it was over and things settled back down, the clerk told Sherry and Laurie to go back to bed, and he spent the rest of the night vacuuming the glass out of their car, and taping a piece of plastic in the broken window. The rest of the trip was cold. Plastic doesn't make a very good wind barrier and it was still winter in this north country.

They arrived at Sherry's parent's house while the family was in church and hid the car. When her parents returned home, Sherry and Laurie were hiding upstairs. As soon as the family came inside, Sherry raced down the stairs. Laurie could hear their joyous reunion from her spot on the stairs. She stood listening and wishing herself away somewhere, anywhere. She was an intruder, and she very much disliked intruding. She lingered on the steps wishing she had stayed at the hotel. But it was too late now, and she didn't want Sherry to think about her. She had come to see her family, so Laurie joined the group in the kitchen as unobtrusively as possible. There were introductions and then Laurie tried to fade into the wood work. They were all going to Sherry's Uncle George's for dinner, and of course Sherry was invited, and, by default, Laurie also. It was a family gathering. She would melt into the background, only speak if spoken to. She had only come to keep Sherry company on the drive down.

Sherry's brother Ken was cute and he kept looking at Laurie. She wished she could read his thoughts. She wasn't trying to intrude on the family; she knew Ken and Sherry were close; she'd stay out of the way. Back home after church, in the evening, Ken, Sherry, and Laurie were sitting in the den, the rest of the family was already in bed. Ken, on a swivel rocker, kept turning so his back was to Laurie. She guessed he wanted to visit with his sister privately. Even though it was early, Laurie excused herself and went to bed.

The plan had been to return home the next day, but now they would be staying until Sherry's car was fixed. They took it to the repair shop early Monday morning, and by late afternoon the window was repaired. Then, Sherry's parents took the family out for supper. Laurie could hardly eat. She felt so guilty for someone paying for her supper. Besides, she ended up sitting beside Ken, and he made her feel very nervous.

Tuesday morning, they were ready to leave and Ken kept hanging around. As they were walking out the door, he looked right at Laurie. "Take care of yourself," he said. She was befuddled, maybe he was feeling guilty that he was glad she was leaving.

It was good to get back to work, where she belonged. Several days passed, and then Friday evening, just before they left the bakery, Sherry cornered Laurie. "Ken called last night. He wonders if you're attached to anyone?" Laurie was speechless. She went home and tried to forget it, but she couldn't. Something about Ken had unsettled her, and apparently he felt the same. For the next week she struggled to not think about him, and did her best to act normal. No more was said, but she knew Sherry was waiting for an answer.

Laurie had the day off Saturday, and her restlessness drove her out of the house. She got in her car and started driving. She had no destination in mind, but she was looking for answers and comfort. The church house drew her, and she turned in that direction. As she drove in the yard, it struck her, this church resembled the one in her dream. She hadn't thought about her dream in a long time and now she paused, remembering. She closed her eyes and pictured it just the way it had always been. A white church, (this one was missing the steeple, but the church looked much the same,) the blue, blue, sky, and utter peace. Laurie let the memories sink into her being, it felt like a balm to her ruffled spirits. After sometime she slowly got out and walked into the church. She was looking for answers, maybe she could find them here. The church was dark. She walked in anyway, and made her way to a bench. She knelt down and tried to pray. She understood that if you really were earnest, God would answer. Laurie wasn't really sure if she knew how you were supposed to know if it was God's voice. But she was going to try. She needed answers.

She knelt there a long time, but there was no revelation, and the dark, quiet church was making her uncomfortable. She walked back out to the car not knowing what else to do. And then she noticed a lane leading to a field behind the church. She walked down the lane and found a place to sit. The grass was a lush, spring green, trees bordered the field on two sides, creating a private sanctuary, with the church just beyond, The sky was a deep, cloudless blue, and as Laurie sat there listening to the quiet of nature, it seemed as though the comfort of her dream again enveloped her. She absorbed it for a long time, and then she looked up at the blue sky and began talking aloud. She didn't understand the feelings she had been experiencing. She had never intended to get married, but if there was a God up there she begged Him to make it plain to her what she was supposed to do. When she left that place the turmoil was gone, and in its place was a conviction that this was right. She didn't love Ken yet, but if a proposal came, she would say yes.

Spring came, and with it the end of school. Laurie flew home the end of May. She had only been home a week when the proposal came, and without hesitation she said yes. Laurie's mother insisted she be home at least six months. So the wedding was planned for fall.

10

The morning of November 11, dawned bright and clear. A perfect fall day in the deep south. Laurie had run the gamut of feelings about this day. As it drew closer she called herself all kinds of a fool for promising to do this. In her heart she knew she shouldn't be getting married, she was not fit to be anyone's wife. And she was deeply afraid of the intimacies that came with marriage. She was not normal, she knew that, but she was trying to do what she felt was right, and to her limited understanding this was it. Ken seemed like a nice person, though she had only seen him twice before this. Still they had talked every week for the last three months, sometimes for two hours at a time. Sherry had assured her, also, that he would treat her good. Besides everyone has a basic need to be loved and Ken seemed to fill that need for her. So she did what she had always done, she quit thinking.

The day had challenges of its own! Laurie had never learned to be comfortable being the center of attention. By three-thirty p.m. they were leaving the church and by four-thirty they were on their way to a motel, and their honeymoon. They weren't going far as they had a long trip back to Ken's home, planned for the end of the week.

Three days, then one day back at Laurie's parents, and by Friday afternoon they headed out. Headed for a new life, in a new place, with new people, far from the scenes of her childhood memories. Laurie never looked back. The first chapter of her life was closed and she had no desire to re-open it. Somewhere deep inside of her there was a faint stirring of hope. Was it possible to make a new start?

Laurie's new home was a trailer house set on a hill, directly across the road from Ken's parents. The yard was full of big old trees she fell in love with immediately. The house was new and it was her own. If only "happily ever after," happened in real life!

At first everything seemed perfect, decorating their own home, getting acquainted, learning to live in a new place. Maybe if Laurie had been any normal girl it would have been perfect. But after the first month, she knew she had made the biggest mistake of her life. It seemed to Laurie that all Ken could think of was the intimacy of marriage. She tried to understand his feelings. Maybe after the new wore off it would be better. But time went on and it only got worse. To her, his actions and demands were opening a door into her past that held only terror and guilt. A door that she had wanted to stay closed forever. The first time it happened, white hot lightening, shot through her. Her brain short-circuited, and she just slipped into survival mode. Don't think, don't feel, just act however he expects. Plaster on a smile, make your voice happy and do what he wants. It became routine. Occasionally Laurie tried to tell him how she felt, but she was not good at explaining her feelings. It *always* turned into a fight. He would explode in anger and tell her she owed it to him. It became worse and worse. The more he demanded the less she felt like giving. She felt like she became his slave and his prisoner.

At first she kept in touch with family and friends. But as time went on she let her friendships go. It was just too hard to pretend to be happily married. Within a year Laurie's mom and sister were the only ones she talked to from her old life. They had an unspoken agreement to call only when they knew Ken would be in the barn, and hang up immediately if she saw him coming. On the rare occasion he caught her on the phone, he would slam doors and stomp around the house muttering and snarling, "Might as well not even have a wife. Why don't you go back and live with mommy?"

Nor was it just her friends. It was the same with his mom and sister. But they didn't know her as well, so it was easier to cover up. Different times they asked her to go shopping, or out to dinner with them. Ken became angry if she asked him if she could go. He said he didn't marry her so he could live alone. So she soon just quit asking, and made up excuses why she couldn't go. It wasn't long until they thought she was just stuck up, and they quit inviting her. One time she went with his mom, and when she got home he was so angry he wouldn't speak to her for a long time. It seemed to Laurie as though he was mad at her all the time! She tried so hard to please him but it was never quite enough.

II

They had been married a little over a year when Laurie became pregnant the first time. Two months before their second wedding anniversary a little girl was born to their home. To Laurie it was a miracle. She really had not believed that God would ever allow her to have a baby of her own. She loved her fiercely, and in the months to come that baby was her life. Three years later another baby was born, this one a boy. After a short stay in the hospital they were discharged to go home.

That first evening at home big sister was so excited and Daddy was so proud! But then Laurie had to change his diaper for the first time. She laid him down on the changing table and as she loosened his diaper, a feeling of revulsion shot through her. She quickly changed him and wrapped him snuggly in his blanket. For two weeks Laurie pushed that horrible feeling away. As long as he was wrapped up she could cuddle and love him all she wanted, but it became harder and harder to ignore her revulsion. And then one day, when the baby was two weeks old, she absolutely could not do it. Laurie laid him down on the changing table to change him, but she froze. She just stood there with her head bowed against the table, as the emotions washed over her. She felt as though she was in a big black hole. Her mind would not function, and when she tried to unpin his diaper, her hands seemed paralyzed. Laurie lost track of time as she fought the waves of revulsion washing over her. Gradually she gained a little control and began searching for options, she came up empty. She was alone in the house with two babies. And no one else would ever understand what she was dealing with. They would think her an unfit mother and take her children away. In her heart she knew she was not fit to be a mother, but no one was going to take her children away!

Laurie stood there with all those thoughts chasing each other around her head, her whole body trembling so she could barely stand. At last in desperation, she fell to her knees beside that changing table, and crying audibly, she prayed, "God, if you want me to take care of this boy you have given me, you will have to give me a love for him." There were no tears, but her chest hurt as though it had been torn open. She knelt there a long time, and slowly she became aware of a quietness, and a tremendous love filled her for that baby. Never again did she feel that revulsion. She got up off her knees, did what needed doing and hugged him tightly to her. In the coming weeks Laurie reflected back on that experience and marveled. There was no doubt that God had answered her desperate plea. Not only did he give her a love for him, he also made him a special little boy! He became Laurie's sunshine.

Laurie loved both of her children fiercely, but there seemed to be a special connection with her boy. He always was the first to pick up on her moods. If she was tired or not feeling well, he would come put his chubby little arms around her and tell her, "Momma, don't be sad." He never was the thoughtless, rambunctious, rough, boy. Oh, he was all boy, alright, but there was always a gentle awareness of the feelings of those around him.

Laurie's life was extremely busy. In addition to taking care of two children and being a housekeeper, she also cleaned houses several days a week, and helped in the barn most evenings. It seemed as though she was always exhausted. And so very lonely, the children were her main companions, and sometimes she longed for an adult to talk to, just about every day things. Laurie felt as though she walked a tight rope with Ken's parents on one side and her family on the other. She didn't dare mention things that happened in her family to Ken, because he told his dad everything. Then his dad would make sarcastic, derogatory remarks about Laurie's family. To Laurie it felt like she was bad, too. She also had to be very careful what she said to her sister as stories had come back to her from clear across the country. Neither could she talk to friends, because there weren't any, and Ken wouldn't have allowed it anyway.

So she bottled everything up inside, the pain from her own family, the abuse from Ken, and all the other stresses that came along. She was determined her children would never see her unhappy, so she kept a smile on her face and made her voice upbeat no matter what she felt inside. But that kind of stress takes its toll. Laurie began having blackout moments; a time when her brain just shut down. Usually it was just momentarily, but it was frightening. She felt out of control, and that only added to the problem. She began having heart palpitations, also. The Dr. did all kinds of tests and finally concluded it was stress. Ken was disgusted, he couldn't imagine what she had to be stressed about.

It became so severe she could no longer hide it from her sister. She became very worried about Laurie and called their dad. He called Uncle Steve and they made a special trip out to visit Laurie. Uncle Steve's stopped in at Ken and Laurie's one afternoon to visit with her, but it was not possible to visit privately, so they instead made plans to meet the next day at the local Dairy Queen. After a very stressful morning, Laurie arrived late for their appointed visit. Uncle Steve wasted no time in getting to the bottom of things. He knew her well enough that she couldn't hide her feelings from him anyway. So she spilled out the whole sordid story. He lost no time in getting in touch with the local minister, and shortly after they made a visit to Ken and Laurie's.

Ken was totally shocked. He had no idea what he was doing was wrong. He also was very angry she had gone behind his back and "tattled" on him. It didn't seem to bother him that he had hurt Laurie. He was just angry he had been found out. However, he was a little more considerate for a while.

Several mornings after this visit, Laurie and the children were eating breakfast, when the phone rang. It was Laurie's mom with the news that Raymond had been killed the night before after an accident in his shop. Laurie hung up the phone and returned to her place at the table in a daze. She leaned her head on her hands, she didn't cry, but she felt as if she was in a black hole and sinking lower by the second. She was losing her grasp on sanity, and she didn't care. But then a little arm stole around her neck and her little boy asked, "Mommy sad?" She clung to him tightly while her mind slowly reeled back from the blackness. Somehow she found the strength to finish readying the children for the day.

When Ken returned she told him about it, his first reaction was, "Oh, your boyfriend." She didn't say another word, just walked away. Later that evening, there was a big fight. He kept taunting her that she loved "precious Raymond" more than him. Words were said, insults hurled, and finally they went to bed, barely on speaking terms. Laurie didn't sleep, she lay there in a kind of stupor. She was numb, too much pain in one day; she couldn't cope with it all. But in the morning Ken surprised her by asking if she wanted to go to the funeral. So arrangements were made for the children to stay with Ken's sister. They left around midnight and drove straight through, twenty-two hours, arriving just in time for the viewing. They stayed at Mark and Marla's, and left immediately following the funeral. But Laurie was so thankful to Ken for taking her. He had been very sweet the whole trip, and seemed to get a little glimpse of the relationship she'd had with Raymond, and actually tried to be very considerate.

Back at home he was soon his old self again, and Laurie had to carefully hide her feelings away. They were not something she wanted to share anyway, she could not bear to have them taunted. Raymond had been one of only three people in the world that she knew, without a doubt, cared about her and would be there if she needed him, no matter what. He was the anchor that kept her from drifting out to sea, and now the rope was cut. For weeks she lived in a void that took all her will power just to put one foot in front of the other. The only thing that kept her going at all was her children. For them she got up in the morning and kept a smile pasted on her face all day.

. . . .

Ken and Laurie had started a home business, and about this time it was starting to really take off. Laurie was finally able to quit her house jobs, but she worked harder than ever. The difference was, she was at home. She also found out she was pregnant again, and as the months passed she began to believe this was God's way of giving her something to live for again. Slowly she began to look forward to life again. In due time another baby was born, this one a girl, and it would be their last. When the baby was three months old they moved to Ken's childhood home. They were buying the farm from his parents.

Their business had grown beyond the two of them, and they now hired part time help. Still Laurie was in the shop nearly all day, every day. She'd go out early, and work for a couple hours before the children got up. Then after getting them up and fed she took the two younger ones out to the shop while the oldest went to school. Ken usually took a nap after breakfast and then came to the shop. Laurie much preferred working alone out there. When Ken came out the stress usually shot way up. She tried to stay on the other side of the shop from him, but it was not always possible. He was not sensitive to her feelings and often his actions were very repulsive. It made her feel dirty and used. She'd take it as long as she could, then try to push him away and get back to work. That always made him angry. He'd accuse her of being a cold fish, and tell her he had his rights; she was his wife. So Laurie mostly bottled it up.

But one day she was particularly weary, the children had been sick, they had been extra busy in the shop, the house was a wreck, and she was at the end of her rope. Ken came in the shop and was again up to his usual thing. She pushed him away. He flew into a rage and called her names that are normally reserved for a female dog. Told her she was just like her mom, and on and on. Laurie ran from the shop, down to the basement to the office, and threw herself on the floor facedown. There were no tears, she didn't even have the strength to cry. She laid there for a long time without moving a muscle. She could have been dead except her heart was still beating. She had no strength to even lift her head. A great black cloud seemed to surround her and weigh her down; no ray of light anywhere. A long time later she began to realize there were little feet running across the floor above her, slowly it dawned on her that it was her babies and they needed her. She tried to move but there was no life in her limbs. In desperation she cried to God and told him if He wanted her to live he was going to have to pick her up off that floor and carry her upstairs. But if he could not do that to just take her home.

Slowly, slowly life began to return to her body, and it almost seemed as though a hand lifted her bodily and set her on her feet. That was a turning point for Laurie. For the next few months she felt as though there was a special Presence holding her, and she clung to that strength.

But it didn't last, the pressure began to build again and she felt herself slipping back into that lonely helpless place. Ken vowed up and down he worshipped her, and Laurie just wished he loved her. She tried to pray, but it seemed to her the more she tried the more demanding Ken became. There was no where to go anymore, no one to turn to, so she finally quit praying. Oh, she didn't tell anyone or quit going to church, or anything so drastic, but in her heart she believed there was no God.

There had been a few times when she thought God had intervened for her, but she decided it was her imagination. It made more sense than trying to believe in a God who was supposedly so loving, but allowed the kind of things she had lived with her whole life, to just continue. She could have sunk a ship with all the unanswered prayers she'd prayed. How many times had she asked for protection and deliverance from the abuse and there were no answers? So that left only two options, either there was no God, or she was some freak of nature that was not a part of the human race. But then why didn't He answer for the sake of her children? She couldn't even care for them properly because she was always just on the verge of collapse. So she decided God didn't exist.

It really didn't make much difference, Laurie would have died before doing anything that would hurt her children, so outwardly nothing changed, except maybe she pulled away from people even more. She really didn't mean to, but there was nothing to talk about; she didn't believe the same things, and it took all her energy to keep a smile in place in public.

12

A new family moved into the community and the congregation.
Laurie didn't pay them any attention, she didn't even bother to meet
them, until one day they walked up and introduced themselves. Brett
and Monica were just a little older than Ken and Laurie. Over the next
two years Monica continued to be-friend Laurie. For a long time Laurie
was polite, but she had no intentions of making friends with a complete
stranger. Monica kept trying, and slowly, slowly Laurie began to return
it a little at a time, until finally they became very good friends.

Brett and Monica were recently returned missionaries trying to
find their place again. Shortly after moving they had applied, and been
approved to be foster parents. After receiving their training they got a
call to take in a brother and sister. The girl was two going on ten, and the
baby was nine months, unable to sit up on his own, or even eat from a
spoon. One evening, a week or two after Brett's got the children, Monica
called and invited Ken's to go out for supper with them. Just the adult's.
The children all stayed at Brett's, and their sixteen year old and Ken's
thirteen year old fixed supper and baby sat.

It was a very enjoyable evening, just two couples with no children.
They talked and laughed and talked some more. Monica shared the
sad details of the little lives they were caring for. The neglect they had
endured tore at Laurie's heart, but nothing prepared her for the reaction
of her first look in that little girls eyes. Instantly she was five again and

all the feelings of betrayal and loneliness and the complete despair, were staring hauntingly back at her. She tried to shut it out, but those eyes followed her and threatened to open doors she had kept closed for years.

That night Laurie lay in bed and cried silently, long into the night. Every time she closed her eyes all she could see was the pain in those little eyes. No one that little should ever look like that! Completely God-forsaken and utterly hopeless. It was the face of the feelings hidden inside Laurie's heart and long ignored.

Morning came and Laurie was still exhausted. She had slept very little and she didn't know how she was going to make it through the day. But somehow she did, and the next, and the next, till after a while she was able to push the memories to the back of her mind and go on. But somehow it was different; they kept coming back at the most inconvenient times. Things she'd forgotten suddenly would resurface a smell or an incident and her body would react in ways she was totally unprepared for.

Then several weeks later Monica called wondering if she could stop in. She needed to talk. So they sat across the table from each other and Monica poured out the story that was emerging of their babies. It was a story of neglect and abuse, both sexually and physically, perpetrated by adults and playmates both. Some of the things Monica described were identical to some of Laurie's own memories.

When Monica left, Laurie's whole body was shaking. She felt like she couldn't breathe; waves of memories washed over her. Things she had pushed away for years, suddenly demanded her attention. It was like a tidal wave and she was helpless to stop it.

Nor did it stop. For weeks Laurie fought those memories. She had never realized before how innocent she would have been. Her mom always made her feel as though she was the one at fault. She had come to believe she was just that bad. In her mind she was bad to the very core. She was lazy and a liar, a talebearer and a prostitute all rolled into one. And she was a murderer, too, because hatred was the same as murder. Anything bad that had happened she believed from the core of her being, had been her fault. But little by little the realization began to immerge that she had been just a little girl when most of the bad things had happened to her.

She began watching her own daughter and she knew there was no way she could have been responsible for the things that happened. Children as young as she had been when the abuse started did not even know about those kinds of things. There was a certain relief in realizing that, but also more confusion, and so much anger! Anger at her brother and his friend for stealing her innocence and ultimately her childhood. Anger at her cousin for stealing her trust in her own ability for friendship. Anger at her mother for allowing it all, even after she knew what was going on, and especially for making her carry the weight of guilt that was not hers. But most of all, anger at a God that would allow such incredible pain. She felt like she was drowning, and there was no life-line anywhere. No one to talk to, no one who cared, no one she trusted, and if she would have found someone to talk to they would not have believed her anyway. She did try to talk to Ken to tell him that she was drowning, but he became angry and told her it was time to forget the past and get over it.

As luck would have it, or was a higher power at work, Mark was scheduled to be one of their revival ministers that year. Laurie counted the days until he arrived, and made sure they were on the list to have the ministers for supper one of the first evenings.

According to custom, after supper the ministers began asking questions, getting a feel of their hearts. Laurie waited patiently while they talked to Ken, and finally when they got around to her, she told them just a little of her struggles. Mark picked up on the direction it was taking them, and wondered if she would like to have a private visit at church the next day. It was arranged for the next afternoon and Laurie met with Mark and one of the home ministers and his wife.

It was hard at first to talk about something that had been suppressed for so long, but Mark knew Laurie's childhood, and little by little he was able to help her open up her heart. She knew Mark cared and nothing she said would change that. It was a relief to finally be able to share her burden with someone she knew wouldn't run as soon as they found out how bad she was. When she walked out of that visit she felt as though the wound that had been festering for so long was open, and now could be cleaned out. It was a long way from clean, and had not even begun to heal, but the process was started.

That night Laurie dreamed, she was standing just inside a little white church. Directly in front of the church, a crossroads met, and in the center of the crossroads a cross stood. The grass around the whole scene was a deep lush green, and above the sky was the bluest blue. Overhead a steeple pointed to heaven and all around and through the dream the words to an old familiar hymn sounded like a benediction, "Behold what love, yes, love divine, the Father showed to thee, In that He gave His only son, thy soul from sin to free. Such love cannot be fathomed, 'Tis like the boundless sea, His broken heart so wounded is bleeding now for thee."

Laurie awoke to a feeling of peace and calm like she had not experienced in years, and as she lay there she remembered her dream. She had nearly forgotten "The Dream"; it was the same one she had dreamed so many times as a child. Then like someone had turned on a light, she realized, that was Jesus, reaching out to her in her darkest hours, comforting her, and holding her in his arms. Through the darkest years of her childhood, that dream was Him speaking to her, and telling her how much He loved her.

It was an incredible feeling, that started at the very core of her being and settled into her heart. The belief that, not only was she loved, but the same one who created the world, had also created her, and she was very special to Him. It shifted her whole belief system about God and her place in life. If He loved her so much that He would take the trouble to reach to her when she didn't even recognize Him, then he must truly have a purpose for her existence. And no matter what she did or didn't do He would always love her. It filled her with a sense of security like she had never experienced before. .

13

When Laurie opened her heart to the Love of God, it also opened another door that she had kept closed. Through all her childhood her feeling towards her mother was a mixture of love and hate. These two opposites sometimes rule in the same heart. Hate is often love betrayed. And it carries with it deepest pain. She had to let go of her self-blame, and place the blame where it belonged. In doing that she was able to free herself and view her life from a different perspective. Not until then did she know the release that comes from forgiving the unforgivable. She needed to forgive those who had wronged and hurt her. And God gave her the grace and strength to do this.

There was still a long way to go. The wounds she had suffered were deep and long standing. They affected all of her life. The way she viewed life and people, and situations, were all colored by her insecurities and the guilt she had carried for so long. Guilt that was not hers. It all had to be re-sorted, based on her new belief that God loved her. It was a long slow process. At first it was so foreign to her to think of herself as a real person. It kept slipping away. She tried so hard to hang onto that peaceful feeling from her dream, but life kept happening and she began checking out again. Not for long, but long enough that she would say things that didn't fit, and end up in places with no memory of how she got there.

Finally her Dr. prescribed a mild anti-depressant and sent her to a counselor. She was diagnosed with Post Traumatic Stress Disorder, PTSD. Which is simply the body saying this is too much, I can't handle it anymore. The anti-depressants simply kept her emotions from fluctuating so severely. Laurie started working through the memories with the help of a counselor and one of her ministers. She found it was necessary to take each incident out of her memory and describe it in detail to someone, along with the feelings it evoked. The counselor helped her to recognize the unhealthy reactions and learn to view things in a more healthy way. One especially helpful exercise the counselor helped her learn, was to imagine a large container of some kind with a lid on the top and a small spout on the bottom. When things happen that threaten to overwhelm her she imagines herself putting them in the barrel and closing the lid. They are still there, but she can give herself permission to put them in the barrel until she feels stronger. Then they can be taken out one at a time and examined. This includes memories and every day happenings that threaten her emotional health.

She found after examining each incident it seems to lose its pain. After several years and many hours talking to someone who could listen impartially, the past has lost its crippling hold on her. The impartial listener was very important, it needed to be someone who had never met her family or Ken. Because she could not be completely open with an acquaintance, she was always protecting their perception of the ones they knew. The scars will be there forever, just like a burn victim or a heart attack, but it is a healed scar that she can live with.

Another part of her healing has involved Ken. Laurie believes God has given her a miracle. She prayed for so many years for deliverance from Ken's demanding control and God has answered. Along with her therapy he has come to understand that she was not trying to push him personally away, but his actions constantly opened old wounds and made them fresh. He's learning to support her when she needs space to work through some new thing that comes up and instead of trying to make her forget the past, he's learned to accept that she will deal with this the rest of her life. He also has learned to recognize the things that trigger unhealthy responses for her and help her work through the feelings or even avoid situations that are unnecessary stresses. And at long last Laurie knows that he does love her. He embraces her problems as tho they are his own. They're learning to talk about their differences instead of silently walking around each other.

Life is beautiful and every time Laurie experiences some small thing for the first time, she marvels how God carried her for so many years. There are so many things like sitting on the floor playing a game, or reaching out and talking to a child, or just looking a person in the eyes when talking to them, that are new to her. She's learned if something goes wrong, or someone is angry, it's not automatically her fault. She can't live by everyone else's whims. She is still trying to learn what she believes, and it is still a struggle to recognize her own likes and dislikes. She lived for so many years doing whatever it took in any given situation, to keep peace. And sometimes it's still easier to just not have an opinion.

These days Laurie spends her time getting acquainted with her own children. She has cared for their physical needs for years, but only now is she able to care for their emotional and spiritual needs. They have been secondary survivors and, as a result they carry some of the same unhealthy thought patterns. They also struggle with insecurities as a result of her years of barely existing, and her guilt complex seems to have rubbed off on them. There is so much truth to the old saying," all work and no play makes jack a dull boy." Laurie's life has been about survival and there was no time for fun and games, so her children have not learned to play either. Together they are trying to learn to enjoy life and to spend time each day just playing! Laurie is also trying to help them learn to express their feelings. That it's ok to be excited or scared and it's ok to let it show. It's also ok, even good, to give hugs and let people know you care! It is her daily prayer that it is not too late to undo the damage that they have inherited. She also contemplates re-connecting with old friends and making new ones. And maybe one day, if God wills, she can help someone else because of what she has been through.

Climb to Healing

A vessel, cracked and broken, was thrown into the gutter,
As I passed by in the street; it seemed to mutter.
"I'm no good at all; I'm dirty and soiled,
My handle is cracked, my pouring spout spoiled.

I'll just hide in the dust, down here for awhile,
Maybe no one will see me, on this side of the pile.
The potter created me beautiful, shiny and clean,
Now my shine is all gone, I feel ugly and mean.

I tried to tell some one I was grossly misused,
But they were sure I was trying to get others abused.
Oh why can't they hear me? I'm crying for help…
But my cry goes unheeded, my heartache unfelt!

But the Master Potter has heard my cry,
And He reaches out to me, I don't know why.
He sent a friend, to pull me out of the pile,
And sometimes in the night, I dream awhile.

My dream is a vision…The Master Potter's house,
And I hear strains of a song, before I rouse.
The Potter loves His creation, He reminds me again.
Though I'm still lost in the pile, because of other's sin.

But now with some help I'm beginning to climb,
From the depth's of the pile, one day at a time.
One step forward and sometimes, two steps back,
Cause memories grip me strong, like a weighted pack.

All the anger and guilt, that were part of my life,
Are beginning to release their strong hold inside.
I'm learning the Master Potter has my good in mind,
As He carefully mends the broken pieces He finds.

And someday I'll look down, from the top of the pile,
Maybe then I'll understand what made the climb worthwhile.
May He bless all who've traveled this journey with me,
And send help to each vessel still broken and weeping.

B.P.S.

Ten Rules For Emotional Health

1. Take care of yourself. Take time to relax , exercise, eat well, spend time with people you enjoy and activities which you find pleasurable. When you are the best; you can be the best that you can in relationships.

2. Choose to find the positives in life experiences instead of focusing on the negatives. Most clouds have a silver lining and offer opportunities for personal growth .When you accept that things are difficult and just do what you need to do , then it doesn't seem so hard.

3. Let go of the past! If you can't change it and you have no control over it then let it go. Don't waste your energy on things that cannot benefit you. Forgive yourself and others.

4. Be respectful and responsible. Don't worry about other people; do what you know is right for you. When you take care of business you feel good. Don't get caught up in blaming others.

5. Acknowledge and take credit for your successes and accomplishments. Avoid false modesty.

6. Take the time to develop one or two close relationships in which you can be honest with your thoughts and feelings.

7. Talk positively to yourself. We talk to ourselves all day long. If we are saying negative and fearful things then that is the way we feel.

8. Remove yourself from hurtful or damaging situations. Temporarily walk away from a situation that is getting out of control. Give yourself some space and problem solve a positive approach to dealing with it.

9. Accept that life is about choices and is always bringing change to you to which requires adjustment.

10. Have a plan for the future. Develop long range goals for yourself , but work in them one day at a time.

A National center for PTSD fact sheet

PTSD and relationships;

Trauma survivors with PTSD often experience problems in their intimate and family relationships or close friendships. PTSD involves symptoms that interfere with trust , emotional closeness, responsible assertiveness and effective problem solving.

Loss of interest in social or sexual activities, and feeling distant from others, as well as feeling emotionally numb. Partners a, friends or family members may feel hurt, alienated, or discouraged, and then become angry or distant toward the survivor.

Feeling irritable, on-guard, easily startled, worried, or anxious may lead the survivors to be unable to relax , socialize, or to be intimate without being tense or demanding. Significant others may feel pressured, tense, and controlled as a result.

Difficulty falling or staying asleep and severe nightmares prevent both the survivor and partner from sleeping restfully, and may make sleeping together difficult.

Trauma memories, trauma reminders, or flashbacks, and the attempt to avoid such memories or reminders, can make living with a survivor feel like living in a war zone or living in constant threat of vague but terrible danger. Living with an individual who has PTSD does not automatically cause PTSD: but it can produce "vicarious" or "secondary" traumatization, which is almost like having PTSD.

Reliving trauma memories, avoiding trauma reminders, and struggling with fear and anger greatly interferes with a survivors' abilities to concentrate, listen carefully, and make cooperative decisions- so problems often go unresolved for a long time. Significant others may come to feel that dialog and teamwork are impossible.

Survivors of childhood sexual and physical abuse, rape, domestic violence, combat or terrorism, genocide, torture, kidnapping or being a prisoner of war , often report feeling a lasting sense of horror, vulnerability and betrayal that interfere with relationships.

Feeling close, trusting, and emotionally or sexually intimate may seem a dangerous "letting down of my guard" because of past traumas- although the survivor often actually feels a strong bond of love or friendship in current healthy relationships.

Having been victimized and exposed to rage and violence, survivors often struggle with intense anger and impulses that usually are suppressed by avoiding closeness or by adopting an attitude of criticism or dissatisfaction with loved ones and friends. Intimate relationships may have episodes of verbal or physical violence.

Survivors may be overly dependent upon or overprotective of partners, family members, friends or support persons (such as healthcare providers and therapists).

Alcohol abuse and substance addiction, as an attempt to cope with PTSD and can destroy intimacy and friendships,

In the first weeks and months following the traumatic event , survivors of disasters, terrible accidents or illnesses, or community violence often feel an unexpected sense of anger, detachment or anxiety in intimate, family and friendship relationships. Most are able to resume their prior level of intimacy and involvement in relationships, but 5-10% who develop PTSD often experience lasting problems with relatedness and intimacy.

Yet many trauma survivors do not experience PTSD, and many couples, families, or friendships with an individual who has PTSD do not experience severe relational problems. Successful intimate relationships require:

Creating a personal support network to cope with PTSD, while maintaining or rebuilding family and friend relationships with dedication, perseverance, hard work, and commitment.

Sharing feelings honestly and openly with an attitude of respect and compassion

Continual practice to strengthen cooperative problem solving and communication.

Infusions of playfulness, spontaneity, relaxation. And mutual enjoyment.

For trauma survivors, .intimate, family and friend relationships are extremely beneficial, providing companionship and belongingness as an antidote to isolation. Self esteem, as an antidote to depression and guilt, opportunities to make a positive contribution to reduce feelings of failure or alienation, and practical and emotional support when coping with life stressors.

As with all psychological disturbances, especially those that impair social, psychological or emotional functioning, it is best to seek treatment from a professional who has expertise in both treating family issues and PTSD. Many therapists with this expertise are members of the International Society for Traumatic Stress Studies, whose membership directory contains a geographical listing indicating those who treat couples or family issues and PTSD. Types of professional help that survivors find helpful for relationships include:

Individual and group psychotherapy for their own PTSD,

Anger and Stress management, and Assertiveness Training,

Couples Communication Classes and Individual and Group Therapies,

Family Education Classes and Family Therapy.

If you need immediate help and don't know where to go here is a resource that is nationally available: RAINN ,Rape, Abuse and Incest National Network (http://www.rainn.org) 1-800-656-HOPE (4673)
You can also call your local crises hotline found in the front pages of your phone book.